W9-BKE-175

Baking With Vegetables

by Rose Deneen

Baking With Vegetables

by Rose Deneen

HenschelHAUS Publishing, Inc.
Milwaukee, Wisconsin

Published by HenschelHAUS Publishing, Inc.
www.henschelHAUSbooks.com

ISBN: 978159598-670-2
E-ISBN: 978159598-671-9
LCCN: 2018954843

Photography by Glenn Carpenter
Food styling by Rosemary Deneen and Glenn Carpenter

Dedication

This cookbook is dedicated to:

The late Elaine Gonzalez, author of *Chocolate Artistry* and a great role model and mentor to me early in my pastry career.

All of my culinary students, who inspire me to think outside the box every day!

Nan Melligan, the first library programmer to have me do a chocolate demonstration at a library over 25 years ago. This launched a side business for me, as I still conduct food demonstrations at libraries all around the suburbs of Chicago.

All those library patrons, who follow me to various libraries who learn something new about food and are supportive of me.

My family, especially Robert and Lynn, who have been supportive during the cookbook writing process and twisting their arms to try some experimental vegetable desserts!

And especially to my fellow chefs—Jeanne, Dean, and Lampros—who inspired me with ideas and tweaks to my recipes.

Thank you all,

Rose Deneen

Contents

Table of Contents

Cookies & Bars

Custards & Mousses

Pastries

Introduction

This cookbook has been a journey of over 25 years—my life as a pastry chef. During my journey, I have baked my share of cakes, cookies, tarts, breads, and much more, and have accumulated and developed some great recipes. I wanted to share some of my favorite recipes, as well as develop some new ones.

The first cake I ever baked was a carrot cake for my father's birthday. He was happy to eat this cake without icing, but I came to love it with cream cheese icing. I was fascinated that I could bake with a vegetable and it tasted great! Like so many other teenagers, I was not a fan of vegetables. However, our food preferences change as we grow older, so I learned to love most vegetables. Thus, the idea for this cookbook was born! We all wish to include more vegetables in our diet, so why not "sneak" veggies in some sweet treats or even a bread?

Many of the recipes are classic (Carrot Cake, Zucchini Bread, Sweet Potato Pie), but you may find recipes that may surprise you (Parsnip Cake, Avocado Chocolate Mousse, Beet Walnut Ginger Bread). I purposely developed recipes using ingredients that would be easy to purchase at your local supermarket. My desire was to make all the recipes approachable, so a variety of recipes use convenience items or ingredients.

I find inspiration at my local supermarkets. I am blessed to have at least six supermarkets within 20 miles of my home and know firsthand where to find both everyday ingredients and those hard-to-find food items. I am always on the lookout for new ingredients (lately vegetables) that would challenge and delight my palate. I hope your journey includes taking the time to bake and enjoy the fruits (or vegetables) of your labor. We never stop learning and/or exploring the food around us and I would believe any chef would agree with this statement.

Happy Baking!

Rose Deneen

Baking
Ingredients

Pumpkin Cinnamon Pecan Ring
(p. 78)

Baking Ingredients

Fat:
I mostly use unsalted butter in my recipes, mostly for great flavor. Use unsalted so you can control the amount of salt in the recipe. Purchase the butter when it's on sale and freeze it.

Sweeteners:
I prefer to use granulated and brown sugars produced with sugar cane versus white sugar beets. Most pastry chefs I know would agree. If the package does not state "Made from Sugar Cane," the sugar is made with sugar beets. And don't forget, brown sugar should always be packed into the measuring cup.

Eggs:
Always use large eggs.

Vanilla Extract:
Don't be cheap! Purchase a good quality, real vanilla, not imitation. Actually, I make my own, which is super easy. Look for the how-to in the My Favorite Recipes chapter.

Flour:
I tested all recipes with unbleached, all-purpose or bread flours. You can use either bleached or unbleached. For gluten-free options, substitute an all-purpose gluten-free mix in most recipes. When measuring into dry measuring cups, remember to spoon flour into cup and level. Do not be tempted to scoop cup into flour; this will likely give you too much flour.

   I experimented with "00" flour for the first time with the Caramelized Onion Focaccia. It's a specialty flour, sometimes found in the Italian food section of some supermarkets in small, two-pound bags. It's a very finely ground white flour, perfect for pasta, pizza dough, or flatbreads like focaccia. It is low in protein, so low gluten development, which results in a soft-textured bread.

Chocolate:
Just like vanilla, don't be cheap! While everyone has a favorite chocolate, only semisweet or dark chocolates work best in pastries. Purchase a good, high-quality chocolate to use in my recipes. How do you know if the chocolate is high quality? Look at the ingredient listing on the package; it should list cocoa butter. If you see other fats, especially palm kernel oil, put it back on the shelf.

Yeast:
All of the yeast bread recipes use "instant" or "fast-rising" yeast so that the bread is ready to eat in around three hours or less!

Vegetables

The following vegetables were used for this cookbook. Please note that I have used various forms of the vegetables (fresh, frozen, or canned). I love the convenience of some produce already peeled and cut into cubes or spirals/noodles.

Many vegetables are seasonal and difficult to find off-season (rhubarb, some squash, and parsnips). However, most of the vegetables utilized in my recipes can be found either fresh, canned, or frozen year round.

Avocado (Spring):

Botanically is considered a fruit because of the pit, it's used as a vegetable. A ripe avocado should be firm, yet yield to gentle pressure.

Beets (Fall):

A red beet puree is used in my recipes. I purchased packaged red baby beets, which are steamed and peeled and ready to eat and easy to puree. You can peel and roast fresh beets, then puree them in a food processor. I also use 100% beet juice in my recipes. Make sure there is no additives, just juice.

Butternut Squash (Winter):

My local grocery store carries fresh butternut squash whole, in pre-packaged cubes, and as pre-packaged spirals. I have used all forms, using a cooked puree in several recipes. The pre-packaged cubes save the time to roast a whole squash, plus you microwave them in the bag. I also found that pulsing the raw spirals/noodles in a food processor created small, riced pieces, which cook during the baking process. If a recipe calls for pumpkin puree, you can substitute butternut squash puree.

Carrots (Summer):

Not only did I use fresh carrots for a few recipes, I also tried using canned honey-carrots in a cookie and was pleasantly impressed! These canned carrots were easy to puree and gave great flavor and moisture to the cookie. And don't forget carrot baby food! It's a great source for a small amount of puree that is 100% vegetable. I use it to make Carrot Ginger Orange pudding, yummy and totally unexpected!

Cauliflower (Fall):

This vegetables was a last minute addition to my cookbook. Cauliflower is so popular right now and can mimic mashed potatoes. Since potatoes can be used in a yeast bread, why not cauliflower? It worked great and tastes wonderful, especially with Parmesan. Look for cauliflower in another unexpected recipe—brownies! I use both frozen mashed and riced cauliflower.

Corn (Summer):

I use frozen corn kernels for a muffin recipe, but you can certainly use a fresh corn cob and remove the kernels.

Garlic (Fall):

For roasting, use a head of white garlic. I also found a company named Gourmet Garden, which sells fresh garlic paste in tubes in the produce section for ease of use. I use the paste in several recipes and am pleased with the flavor.

Onions (Summer):

I use yellow, white sweet onions, as well as shallots. There are times when you can substitute shallots for onions, but for the Caramelized Onion Focaccia, stick to yellow or white onions.

Parsnips (Spring):

Fresh parsnips look like light brown carrots, but have a taste similar to sweet potatoes. I handle then just like carrots in terms of peeling, then grating them for a cake. Again, an unexpected surprise!

Poblano Peppers (Year Round):

Poblano peppers are deep green with smooth, glossy skins, thick walls and an elongated, somewhat curved shape. They have an earthy, spicy flavor. They should always be roasted or cooked; do not eat raw.

Pumpkin (Fall):

A puree is used in my recipes. You can simply purchase canned pumpkin puree (not pie filling) or roast a sugar pie pumpkin during the Fall/Winter season and puree the cooked flesh. I tested all the pumpkin recipes with both fresh and canned purees. I also stumbled upon a Butterkin Squash last fall and loved it (roast it the same way as you would a sugar pumpkin). It worked well in recipes using pumpkin. Also, if a recipe calls for Butternut Squash puree, you can substitute pumpkin puree.

To roast a sugar pumpkin, preheat oven to 350°F. Place whole pumpkin in microwave and heat on HIGH for 3 minutes (this softens the skin to make cutting the pumpkin in half much easier). Place pumpkin on cutting board. Using a serrated bread knife, cut in half, from top to bottom, cutting next to the stem (sometimes the stem becomes soft and you can remove it). Place each half, flesh side down, on a parchment-lined sheet pan. Leave the seeds in place; they become much easier to remove once roasted. Roast in oven 35 to 50 minutes, depending on the pumpkin size. A fork inserted should move easily through skin and flesh. Remove from oven, cool, remove seeds and skin. Puree the flesh in food processor. Refrigerate until ready to use, up to five days.

Red Peppers (Year Round):

Roasted red peppers add great flavor to my savory cheesecake. You can roast fresh red peppers or used jarred peppers that just need chopping. I tested both methods and the results tasted the same.

Rhubarb (Spring):

While rhubarb is botanically a vegetable, it's treated more like a fruit. It's a very seasonal fruit (April through June). I had a tough time finding it frozen off-season. So, enjoy it while you can! Try roasting it in the oven, following my Roasted Rhubarb and Strawberry Shortcakes recipe. Yummy!

Rutabaga (Year Round):

This vegetable was not on my initial list for the cookbook, but I saw it on the grocery shelf in a can, so I thought, why not? It actually worked great in a bread pudding. It's a wonderful way for everyone to perhaps eat a new vegetable.

Spinach (Spring):

Frozen, chopped spinach is used in this cookbook.

Sweet Potato (Fall):

Because of the popularity of this potato, it's easy to find off-season. I used a variety of this potato for recipe development, including the common orange-flesh sweet potato, the Red Garnet variety, and canned yams (technically sweet potatoes). If the recipe states, "sweet potato puree," any potato can be used. However, I have a couple of recipes where I preferred the canned yams over baked potato puree. The canned potatoes are easy to puree and use immediately. There are some stores that carry canned, pureed sweet potatoes, so check the shelves.

    For more information about the differences between yams and sweet potatoes, check out www.americansweetpotato.org

Tomatoes (Summer):

I have just one recipe using tomatoes, specifically tomato juice.

Zucchini (Summer):

This easy to find summer squash adds moisture, texture and flavor to your baked goods. It is also easy to grate, so I found it easy to add to a chocolate cake mix and no one will know it's there!

My Favorite Baking Tools

The following tools and supplies are items I have used for over 25 years throughout my baking career, as well as items used in this cookbook. You do not have to purchase these items to be successful, but they make the prepping and baking process SO MUCH easier.

Metal Bench Scraper
Invaluable tool for a number of applications from cutting yeast dough into portions to simply scraping the work table of crumbs, flour, etc.

Silicone Prep/Baking Mats
I use these mats for a variety of tasks from kneading my yeast doughs to baking cookies on them.

Heatproof Bowl Spatulas
This all-purpose tool is necessary for scraping bowls and works great when making candies.

Small Offset Icing Spatulas
Another invaluable tool for spreading batters in pans, spreading icing on cakes, and so much more!

Digital Thermometer
This should be a kitchen staple for checking internal temperatures of meats, poultry and breads.

Digital Scale
The scale should also be a kitchen staple; purchase a scale that will measure at least 5 pounds and as little as 0.1g.

Food Processor
It is difficult to make a vegetable puree without this countertop appliance.

Mini Food Chopper
Great for chopping a small quantity of nuts.

Kitchenaid Stand Mixer
Do I really have to explain this one? I have had this red one for over 25 years!

Veggie Mousse Éclairs
(recipe p. 59)

My
Favorite
Recipes

Chocolate Glaze

I have been using this glaze since my first pastry job. My supervisor had attended Le Cordon Bleu in France, so I believe this was one of his recipes from school. I use the glaze for éclair icing, cake glaze, and brownie glaze. It's one of the few recipes still in my head, as it's simple to remember and simple to prepare. Leftovers keep well in the refrigerator for up to 1 month.

6 ounces (1½ sticks) butter, cut into smaller pieces
¼ cup light corn syrup
¼ cup water
12 ounces high-quality semisweet chocolate, roughly chopped

Place butter, corn syrup and water in medium saucepan and heat until butter is melted and just about boiling, stirring occasionally. Remove pan from heat and add chocolate; whisk to combine until chocolate is melted and mixture becomes smooth.

Keep leftover glaze in covered container refrigerated up to 1 month.

Variations:
Coffee: Add 1 tbsp. instant coffee to hot butter mixture before adding chocolate.
Orange: Replace water with orange juice.

Cream Cheese Frosting

I first saw this alternative mixing method in Cook's Illustrated and realized it produced a nice, thick frosting. Traditional creaming methods tended to make a very soft frosting; this method keeps the frosting thick and easy to frost a cake.

¼ pound (1 stick) butter, softened
2 cups confectioner's sugar
2 pkgs. (8 ounce each) cream cheese, softened and cut into pieces
1 tsp. vanilla extract
Pinch salt

Beat butter and sugar in mixer bowl on medium speed for 2 minutes or until smooth and fluffy. On low speed, gradually add pieces of cream cheese. Scrape down bowl; add vanilla and salt. Beat until blended well.

Variation:
Add grated zest from one orange into prepared frosting.

Homemade Vanilla Extract

Making your own vanilla is worth the time and effort. Use a combination of vanilla beans if desired.

2 cups vodka
1 pint bottle with resealable lid
3 to 4 vanilla beans (Madagascar, Tahitian or Mexican)

Pour vodka into bottle. Place vanilla beans onto a cutting board and using a sharp, paring knife, cut down the middle of each bean to expose the seeds. If the beans are taller than the jar, cut in half horizontally. Place all cut beans into vodka. Close bottle, place in dark, cool cabinet and let infuse for 2 to 3 weeks.

The vanilla beans will keep infusing flavor into new vodka added to bottle; I add more when the bottle is more than ½ empty. Replace or add more beans after 9 to 12 months.

Éclairs

This is a classic recipe for éclair or pate a choux. I like to pipe them smaller, so the finished éclair is 2 to 3 bites. Bread flour is preferred, but you can substitute with all-purpose flour.

1 cup water
¼ pound (1 stick), butter, cut into pieces
1 tbsp. granulated sugar
½ tsp. salt
1 cup bread flour
4 eggs

Large pastry bag
Large star or round decorating tip

Preheat oven to 350°F. Line a large sheet pan with parchment paper.

Bring water, butter, sugar, and salt to a rapid boil in a medium saucepan over medium heat. Make sure butter is completely melted. Reduce heat slightly and add all of the flour at once. Stir constantly to bring mixture together to form a ball of dough; cook for 1 more minute. Remove from heat and move dough to mixer bowl. Use paddle attachment and beat dough on low speed to cool for 2 minutes.

Add the eggs to the dough, one at a time, mixing on low speed for about 30 seconds or when dough absorbs the egg. After mixing in the last egg, stop mixer and scrape down bowl and paddle. Mix on low to blend well; dough should look smooth and shiny.

Insert decorating tip into pastry bag and fill with ½ of dough mixture. Pipe 3x1-inch éclairs onto parchment-lined sheet pan. Bake 45 to 50 minutes or until éclairs are golden brown. Do not open oven for the first 30 minutes, otherwise éclairs may collapse.

Cool completely before filling. Fill and glaze as desired.

Makes (24) 3-inch éclair shells.

Pie Dough

This dough is easy to make and by grating the stick of cold butter, no mixers or food processors needed!

3 cups all-purpose flour
2 tsp. granulated sugar
1 tsp. salt
¼ pound (1 stick) cold butter
½ cup (½ stick) white shortening stick, frozen and cut into pieces
½ to ¾ cup ice water

Place flour, sugar and salt in medium bowl. Grate cold butter stick over flour, using a cheese grater. Add frozen shortening and mix together with hands to evenly distribute fat. Make a well in the center to the bottom of the bowl and add ½ cup water. Mix with hands, adding a little more water until dough feels moist and easily comes together. Knead the dough a few times and flatten into a disc. Wrap in plastic and refrigerate for at least 1 hour or overnight.

Roll out half of the dough on a lightly floured surface into a ¼-inch thick and at least 12-inch round. Fold dough in half and place into pie pan. Unfold dough and push into place. Using kitchen scissors, trim excess dough, leaving about 1-inch around top to create edging. Fold dough about ½-inch down and create desired edging design. Place pie pan into refrigerator for at least 30 minutes.

Makes enough dough for (1) double-crust pie or (2) single-crust pies.

Variation:
Eliminate or reduce sugar if dough is used for savory pies, such as quiche.

Candied Carrot Curls

These fun, edible decorations are easy to prepare and taste great!

1 cup granulated sugar
1 cup water
2 medium carrots

Equipment needed: Y-shaped vegetable peeler, silicone mat, and sheet pan

Preheat oven to 250°F. Place silicone mat on sheet pan; set aside.

Bring sugar and water to a boil in a large, wide sauté pan. Meanwhile, peel the outer skin of the carrots. Peel long strips of carrots, starting at the top. Once sugar mixture is boiling, reduce heat to a simmer and add carrot strips, laying them flat individually. Simmer carrots 8 minutes; use tongs to remove the carrots. Place carrot strips flat on prepared sheet pan. Bake 30 minutes, then use tongs to turn over strips. Bake 20 minutes and remove from oven. Peel strips from silicone one at a time and wrap around rounded handle of a spoon to create a curl. Place curls onto silicone mat and bake another 20 minutes (curls should keep their shape). Turn off oven and let curls sit overnight in cooled oven.

Variation: Candied Walnuts
Replace the carrots with 1 cup whole walnut pieces. Simmer in sugar mixture for only 4 minutes. Bake for 1 hour at 250°F on silicone mat, turning over halfway through.

I have prepared both candied carrot curls and walnuts at the same time. Simmer the carrots for 8 minutes first, remove from sugar mixture, then add walnuts and simmer 4 minutes. Place both on silicone mat and bake following the candied carrot procedure.

Streusel Topping

I have been using this streusel for over 25 years. It's great in a variety of baked goods, including fruit crisps, bar cookie topping and crumb cake topping.

½ cup all-purpose flour
½ cup light or dark brown sugar
¼ pound (1 stick) cold butter, cut into pieces
½ cup oats
½ cup nuts (pecans, walnuts or almonds)

Place flour and brown sugar in food processor bowl; pulse to combine. Add butter and pulse until butter is cut into small pieces. Add oats and nuts; pulse to chop nuts and combine.

Store topping covered in refrigerator for up to 2 months.

Makes 2½ cups streusel.

Sweet Potato
Streusel Swirl Cake
(p. 26)

Mini Maple-Glazed Pumpkin Cakes
(p. 22)

Carrot Cake
(p.21)

Cakes

Carrot Cake

This is the first cake I ever made. I was a teenager and baked it for my dad's birthday. It was his favorite cake and he never wanted frosting on it. I also made it for his last birthday before he passed from Parkinson's. I have made this cake at every restaurant and catering pastry job I ever held and still make it with my culinary students every semester. I still have not found anyone who doesn't love this cake! And honestly, it's so moist, no frosting is needed. However, cream cheese frosting is also great with this cake; look for my recipe on page 13. Also try the variation noted below, using butternut squash for the carrots!

1 pound carrots, peeled and grated
   (larger grate on a box grater), about 4 cups
1 cup chopped walnuts
1 cup raisins
4 eggs
1 cup granulated sugar
1 cup dark brown sugar

1¼ cup vegetable oil
1 tbsp. vanilla extract
2 cups all-purpose flour
1 tbsp. baking powder
1 tbsp. ground cinnamon
1 tsp. baking soda
1 tsp. salt

Preheat oven to 350°F. Spray (2) 9-inch round cake pans with non-stick spray and line bottoms with parchment paper rounds. Or spray a 13x9x2-inch pan with non-stick spray (I usually serve the cake right from this pan, so no need for parchment paper).

Combine the carrots, walnuts, and raisins in a medium bowl; set aside. Whisk the eggs in a large bowl. Whisk in both sugars, oil, and vanilla. Place flour, baking powder, cinnamon, baking soda, and salt on top of egg mixture and fold in JUST until mixed. Fold in carrot/walnut mixture. Divide cake batter between the (2) 9-inch pans or pour all the batter into the 13x9x2-inch pan.

Bake the round cakes 35 to 40 minutes or the 13x9x2-inch pan 40 to 45 minutes, making sure a toothpick inserted into the center comes out clean. Place hot pans on cooling rack; let cool about 10 minutes. Loosen round cakes from edges with a knife and invert to cool completely. Or let cake cool completely in 13x9x2-inch pan.

Makes (1) 2-layer cake or (1) 13x9x2 cake, 12 to 15 servings.
Decorate with Candied Carrot Curls and Candied Walnuts (see page 16 for recipe).

Tip: *If the raisins are dry, soak them in hot water for 5 to 10 minutes; drain the water. This will rehydrate the raisins and help keep the cake moist.*

Tip: *Vegetable oil can be replaced with canola, corn, or even a light baking olive oil.*

Variation: *Replace grated carrots with about 12 ounces fresh butternut squash spirals, pulsed in food processor to small, riced pieces; measure out 3 cups.*

Mini Maple-Glazed Pumpkin Cakes

Craving some cake? These mini, yummy cakes are fast to prep, quick to bake, and simple to glaze.

Cake:
1 cup all-purpose flour
½ tsp. baking soda
½ tsp. baking powder
½ tsp. salt
½ tsp. ground cinnamon
¼ tsp. ground ginger
¼ pound (1 stick) butter, softened
½ cup granulated sugar
2 eggs
⅔ cup pumpkin puree
½ tsp. vanilla extract
½ tsp. maple extract

Icing:
1½ cups confectioners' sugar
1 tbsp. light corn syrup
½ tsp. maple extract
Warm water

Preheat oven to 350°F. Butter and flour a 6-cavity mini tube pan; set aside.

Prepare cake:
Whisk together flour, baking soda, baking powder, salt, cinnamon and ginger in small bowl; set aside. Beat butter and sugar in electric mixer bowl with paddle on medium speed for 2 minutes. Add eggs, one at a time, mixing well after each egg. Add puree and both extracts; beat well. Add flour mixture all at once; mix on low speed just until blended. Using a bowl spatula, mix the batter by hand to ensure the batter is well-blended.

Divide batter into prepared pan, about ⅓ cup batter into each cavity. Tap pan onto counter to remove air bubbles. Bake 18 to 20 minutes or until toothpick inserted into center comes out clean. Place pan on cooling rack for 10 minutes.

Prepare icing:
Whisk together sugar, corn syrup, maple extract and about 1 tbsp. water. Icing should be fairly thick and will thin as you glaze the warm cakes. If too thick, add a little more water.

Invert pan onto cooling rack to remove cakes. Place a piece of parchment paper underneath rack to catch extra icing. Spoon icing onto warm cakes. Cool cakes about 15 more minutes before serving.

Makes 6 servings.

Zucchini Chocolate Cake

Perhaps there is a small zucchini left in the fridge and not sure what to do with it? Grate it and add it to a packaged cake mix. The darkness of the cake "hides" the veggies, but adds a nice texture. The use of coffee in place of water intensifies the chocolate flavor.

1 cup grated zucchini
½ cup chopped pecans or walnuts
1 cup room temperature coffee
1 tsp. ground cinnamon
1/3 cup light olive oil
3 eggs
1 box (15.25 ounce) Devil's Food cake mix
½ recipe Chocolate Glaze, cooled slightly (page 12)

Preheat oven to 350°F. Spray a 10-cup tube pan with nonstick cooking spray.

Combine zucchini and pecans in small bowl; set aside.

Combine coffee, cinnamon, oil, eggs and cake mix in electric mixer bowl. Beat on low speed for 30 seconds. Beat on medium speed for 2 minutes. Fold in zucchini and pecans. Pour batter into prepared pan. Bake 38 to 42 minutes or until toothpick inserted into center comes out clean.

Cool cake in pan on cooling rack for 10 minutes. Invert pan and remove cake to cool. To apply glaze to cake, place parchment paper under cooling rack, spoon warm glaze over top of warm cake, and let it drip over sides of cake. Cool cake completely before serving.

Serve cake at room temperature. Store cake in refrigerator for up to 3 days.

Makes 12 servings.

Tip: *Room temperature water can be used in place of coffee.*

double recipe to use full can of sweet potatoes

Sweet Potato Crumb Cakes

I love crumb cakes, but it's hard to find them in bakeries. So, once I found the crumb cake pan, I had no excuse but to make my own cakes!

Cake:
1 can (15 to 20 ounce) sweet potatoes in syrup
1½ cups all-purpose flour
½ tsp. baking soda
½ tsp. baking powder
½ tsp. salt
½ tsp. ground cinnamon
¼ pound (1 stick) butter, softened
¾ cup granulated sugar
2 eggs
¼ cup plain Greek yogurt or sour cream
1 tsp. vanilla extract

Streusel: Prepare Streusel Topping from page 17

one batch sufficient for double cakes

Preheat oven to 350°F. Spray a 12-cavity, nonstick crumb cake pan (with removable bottoms) with nonstick spray; set aside.

Drain potatoes, reserving the syrup. Place potatoes and 2 tbsp. reserved syrup in small bowl and mash, using a potato masher or fork. Measure out ¾ cup puree. Whisk together the flour, baking soda, baking powder, salt and cinnamon in a small bowl; set aside.

Beat butter in electric mixer bowl on medium speed for 30 seconds. Add sugar and continue beating on medium speed for 2 minutes. Scrape down bowl; continue beating on medium-low speed and gradually add eggs, 1 at a time, beating for about 30 seconds after each addition. Scrape down bowl. Add ½ of flour mixture, potato puree, yogurt and vanilla; beat on low until combined. Add remaining flour mixture all at once and beat on low until just combined. Remove from mixer and hand mix with bowl spatula to make sure all ingredients are blended well.

Measure about ⅓ cup of the cake batter into each prepared pan cavity; spread evenly. Divide and sprinkle streusel even onto each cake. Bake 26 to 28 minutes or until a toothpick inserted into center of cakes comes out clean. Cool 10 minutes in pan, then push up onto bottom of each cavity to remove cake and place on cooling rack.

Keep covered at room temperature for up to 3 days.

Makes 12 crumb cakes.

Sweet Potato
Crumb Cakes

Sweet Potato Streusel Swirl Cake

This moist cake marries a sweet potato spice cake with a pecan and orange streusel.

Cake:
3 cups all-purpose flour
1 tsp. baking soda
1 tsp. baking powder
1 tsp. salt
1 tsp. pumpkin pie spice
½ pound (2 sticks) unsalted butter, softened
1½ cups granulated sugar
4 eggs
1½ cups sweet potato puree
½ cup sour cream or plain Greek yogurt
2 tsp. vanilla extract

Streusel:
½ cup all-purpose flour
½ cup light brown sugar
1 cup finely chopped pecans, divided
1 tbsp. finely grated orange zest (1 orange)
½ tsp. ground cinnamon
¼ tsp. salt
4 tbsp. (½ stick) butter, melted

Icing:
2 cups confectioners' sugar
¼ cup fresh orange juice (squeezed from
    zested orange from streusel)

Preheat oven to 350°F. Spray a 10-cup, nonstick fluted tube pan with nonstick spray; set aside.

Prepare streusel:
Mix flour, sugar, ½ cup pecans, zest, cinnamon, salt, and melted butter in a medium bowl until well blended; set aside.

Prepare cake:
Whisk together the flour, baking soda, baking powder, salt and spice in a small bowl; set aside.

Beat butter in electric mixer bowl on medium speed for 30 seconds. Add sugar and continue beating on medium speed for 3 minutes. Scrape down bowl; continue beating on medium-low speed and gradually add eggs, 1 at a time, beating for about 30 seconds after each addition. Scrape down bowl. Add ½ of flour mixture, potato puree, sour cream, and vanilla; beat on low until combined. Add remaining flour mixture all at once and beat on low until just combined. Remove from mixer and hand mix with bowl spatula to make sure all ingredients are well blended.

Scoop ½ of the cake batter into prepared pan; spread evenly. Sprinkle streusel evenly onto batter. Scoop remaining batter onto streusel; spread evenly. Bake 55 to 60 minutes or until a toothpick inserted into center comes out clean. Cool 10 minutes in pan, the invert to remove cake onto a cooling rack.

Prepare Icing:
Whisk confectioners' sugar and orange juice in a small bowl to make a thick icing. Drizzle over warm cake. Decorate with remaining ½ cup pecans. Cool completely before serving. Keep cake covered at room temperature up to 3 days.

Makes 12 servings.

Parsnip Spice Cake

The parsnip is treated like carrots in a carrot cake. When you use a cake mix, this cake comes together quickly. The parsnips give a great flavor and texture to this spice cake. Top the cake with Cream Cheese Frosting (page 13) for a yummy and unusual dessert!

8 ounces fresh parsnips, peeled and grated to measure 2 cups
¾ cup raisins
1 cup chopped walnuts
1 box (15.25 ounce) spice cake mix, plus ingredients to prepare mix

Preheat oven to 350°F. Spray a 13x9x2-inch baking pan with nonstick spray.

Place parsnips, raisins and walnuts in medium bowl; set aside.

Prepare cake mix following package directions. Stir in parsnip/raisin mixture. Pour batter into prepared pan and bake 30 to 35 minutes or until toothpick inserted into center comes out clean. Cool cake completely before serving or topping with frosting. Without frosting, cake can be covered at room temperature for up to 3 days. If frosted, refrigerate covered for up to 3 days.

Makes 15 servings.

Rhubarb Upside-Down Strawberry Cake

This cake is a lovely way to enjoy the classic flavors of rhubarb and strawberries. By using a cake mix, this cake comes together quickly. The strawberry glaze on top gives a great burst of strawberry flavor and keeps the rhubarb moist. A yellow cake mix can be substituted for the strawberry cake.

4 tbsp. (½ stick) butter, melted
2/3 cup light brown sugar
1 pound (3 cups) sliced fresh or frozen (thawed) rhubarb
Pinch salt
1 box (15.25 ounce) strawberry cake mix, plus ingredients to prepare mix
½ cup strawberry jam
1 tbsp. water

Preheat oven to 350°F. Spray a 13x9x2-inch pan with nonstick spray. Pour melted butter into pan and tilt to spread evenly. Sprinkle on brown sugar and top with rhubarb, spreading fruit single layer. Sprinkle rhubarb with salt.

Prepare cake mix following package directions. Gently pour batter onto rhubarb; spread evenly. Bake 32 to 35 minutes or until a toothpick inserted into center comes out clean.

Cool cake in pan 5 minutes. Loosen cake from sides of pan with a knife. Turn pan upside down on cooling rack, placing a sheet of parchment paper underneath rack to catch crumbs and/or juice.

Heat jam and water in small saucepan, stirring to break up jam. Brush jam liberally on top of rhubarb. Cool cake completely before serving. Serve with whipped cream or vanilla ice cream.

Store cake covered at room temperature for up to 3 days.

Makes 15 servings.

Pumpkin Crumble
Bars (p. 39)

Double Chocolate
Beet Cookies
(p. 35)

Sweet Potato
Whoopie Pies
(p. 37)

Cookies &
Bars

Butternut Squash Cookies

Spiral vegetables are available in most produce sections of the grocery store. Processing the spirals into tiny riced pieces provides a great flavor and texture and of course, vegetables in a cookie!

1 container (12 ounce) raw butternut squash
    spirals
⅔ cup chopped pecans or walnuts
⅔ cup dried cranberries or raisins
2 cups all-purpose flour
1½ cups old-fashioned oats
2 tsp. ground cinnamon
1 tsp. salt
1 tsp. baking powder

½ tsp. baking soda
½ tsp. ground ginger
½ pound (2 sticks) butter, softened
1 cup dark brown sugar
½ cup granulated sugar
2 eggs
1½ tsp. vanilla extract

Preheat oven to 375°F. Line (2) sheet pans with parchment paper.

Place squash spirals in food processor and pulse several times to create small riced pieces. Measure 3 cups and place in small bowl with pecans and cranberries; set aside.

Combine flour, oats, cinnamon, salt, baking powder, baking soda and ginger; set aside.

Beat butter in electric mixer bowl on medium speed until creamy, about 30 seconds. Add both sugars; beat on medium speed for 2 minutes. Scrape down bowl and add eggs, one at a time, mixing about 30 seconds after each egg. Add vanilla; blend well. Add flour/oat mixture and blend on low speed until blended well. Beat in squash/pecan mixture.

Scoop onto prepared sheet pans, leaving about 1 inch between for spreading. Bake 16 to 18 minutes until light golden brown.

Store baked cookies in airtight container for up to 5 days or freeze for longer storage.

Makes about 40 2-inch cookies

Variation: For bar cookies, prepare cookie dough as noted above and spread into a 13x9x2-inch pan (sprayed with non-stick spray). Bake at 350°F for 30 to 35 minutes or until golden brown.

Makes 18 bar cookies.

Caramelized Cauliflower Chocolate Brownies

Yes, believe it or not, caramelized cauliflower pairs well with chocolate. This pairing is a result of the Maillard reaction, which caramelizes the natural sugars in the vegetable. I got the idea for this brownie after referencing one of my favorite books, "The Flavor Bible."

8 ounces (2 sticks) butter
4 ounces semisweet chocolate, chopped
3 tbsp. unsweetened cocoa powder
1 cup granulated sugar
3 eggs
1 tsp. vanilla extract
½ cup caramelized riced cauliflower, at room temperature
½ cup all-purpose flour
½ tsp. salt

Preheat oven to 325°F. Spray a 9-inch square pan with nonstick spray. For easier removal of baked brownies, line pan with pieces of parchment paper that extend over the top of pan to create handles. Lightly spray parchment paper; set aside.

Melt butter in medium glass bowl in microwave. Add chocolate and cocoa powder; whisk until chocolate melts. Let cool slightly. Whisk in sugar, then whisk in eggs and vanilla. Stir in cauliflower, flour and salt. Pour batter into prepared pan and bake 30 to 34 minutes or until toothpick inserted into center comes out fairly clean.

Cool brownies in pan, lift up parchment paper handles to remove from pan. Store brownies in airtight container at room temperature for up to 5 days or freeze for longer storage.

Makes 12 servings.

Caramelized Cauliflower

1 pkg. (12 ounce) frozen, riced cauliflower
2 tbsp. butter
1 tbsp. olive oil
Pinch salt

Remove cauliflower from freezer to thaw slightly, about 20 minutes. Heat butter and oil in medium sauté pan over medium heat. When hot, add cauliflower and stir and cook until cauliflower begins to brown well, about 6 to 8 minutes. Transfer to plate to cool.

Carrot Cake Cookies

Now your favorite oatmeal cookie has a vegetable baked right into it, making you feel a little better about indulging. This recipe makes about 40 cookies; leftover cookies freeze well in an airtight container.

1 can (15 ounce) sliced honey carrots
2¼ cups all-purpose flour
1 cup old-fashioned oats
2 tsp. ground cinnamon
1 tsp. salt
1 tsp. baking powder
½ tsp. baking soda

¼ tsp. ground ginger (optional)
½ cup raisins
½ cup chopped walnuts
½ pound (2 sticks) butter, softened
1 cup dark brown sugar
½ cup granulated sugar
2 eggs
1 tsp. vanilla extract

Preheat oven to 375°F. Line (2) sheet pans with parchment paper.

Drain canned carrots; use potato masher or fork to mash into a puree; set aside.

Stir together flour, oats, cinnamon, salt, baking powder, baking soda and ginger in medium bowl. Add raisins and walnuts; toss to coat with flour mixture. Set aside.

Beat butter in electric mixer bowl on medium speed until creamy, about 30 seconds. Add both sugars; beat on medium speed for 2 minutes. Scrape down bowl, then add eggs, one at a time, beating about 30 seconds after each addition. Add vanilla and carrot puree; beat well (mixture will look slightly curdled). Add flour/raisin mixture and blend on low speed until blended well.

Scoop onto prepared sheet pans, leaving about 1 inch between for spreading. Bake 15 to 17 minutes or until light golden brown.

Store baked cookies in airtight container up to 5 days or freeze for longer storage.

Makes about (40) 2-inch cookies.

Variation:
Carrot Cake Sandwich Cookies: Prepare one recipe of Cream Cheese Frosting on page 13 or purchase canned frosting. Sandwich two cookies together with frosting. Keep sandwich cookies refrigerated.

Double Chocolate Beet Cookies

The beet puree gives an underlying flavor that compliments the chocolate. I love using mini chocolate chips so there is chocolate in every bite!

2⅓ cup all-purpose flour
¼ cup unsweetened cocoa powder
1 tsp. baking soda
1 tsp. salt
½ pound (2 sticks), butter, softened
1 cup light brown sugar

½ cup granulated sugar
2 eggs
1 tsp. vanilla extract
½ cup beet puree
1 pkg. (10 ounce) mini semisweet chocolate chips
¾ cup chopped walnuts

Preheat oven to 375°F.

Combine flour, cocoa powder, baking soda and salt in small bowl; set aside.

Beat butter on medium speed in electric mixer for 30 seconds. Add brown sugar and granulated sugar; beat on medium for 2 minutes. Scrape down bowl and add eggs, one at a time, mixing about 30 seconds after each egg. Add vanilla and puree; beat well (mixture may look a little curdled). Add flour mixture and beat on low speed just until combined. Add chocolate chips and nuts; blend well.

Scoop cookie dough onto parchment-lined sheet pans, leaving about 1 inch between for spreading. Bake 14 to 16 minutes. Let cool on pans 5 minutes, then transfer to cooling rack.

Store cookies in airtight container for up to 5 days or freeze for longer storage.

Makes 36 cookies.

Pumpkin Butterscotch Brownies

These brownies are quick to make in one bowl. They are wonderfully moist and the butterscotch chips give them a marvelous flavor. White chocolate chips can be substituted and taste yummy as well.

¼ pound (1 stick) butter
1 cup dark brown sugar, packed
1 egg
¾ cup pumpkin puree
1 tsp. vanilla extract
1 cup all-purpose flour
½ tsp. baking powder
½ tsp. baking soda
½ tsp. salt
½ pkg. (11 ounce) butterscotch-flavored chips, about ¾ cup
½ cup chopped pecans

Preheat oven to 350°F. Spray a 9-inch square pan with nonstick spray. For easier removal of baked brownies, line pan with pieces of parchment paper that extend over the top of pan to create handles. Lightly spray parchment paper; set aside.

Melt butter in medium glass bowl in microwave. Whisk in brown sugar; then whisk in egg, pumpkin and vanilla. Add flour, baking powder, baking soda, salt; stir to blend. Fold in butterscotch chips and pecans. Spread batter into prepared pan.

Bake 25 to 30 minutes or until toothpick inserted into center comes out mostly clean. Cool completely before serving.

Store covered at room temperature up to 5 days or freeze for longer storage.

Makes 16 brownies.

Sweet Potato Whoopie Pies

These fun, cakelike cookies are yummy on their own. However, sandwich a marshmallow frosting in between two cookies and you are likely to say "Whoopie"!

Whoopie Pies:
2¼ cups all-purpose flour
2 tsp. ground cinnamon
1 tsp. salt
1 tsp. baking powder
½ tsp. baking soda
½ tsp. ground ginger
½ pound (2 sticks) butter, softened
1 cup light brown sugar
½ cup granulated sugar
1 egg
1 tsp. vanilla extract
¾ cup sweet potato puree

Frosting:
¼ pound (1 stick) butter, softened
1½ cups confectioners' sugar
1 jar (7.5 ounce) marshmallow crème
1 tsp. vanilla extract
Pinch salt

Preheat oven to 350°F. Line (2) sheet pans with parchment paper.

Prepare whoopie pies:
Stir together flour, cinnamon, salt, baking powder, baking soda and ginger in small bowl; set aside.

Beat butter in electric mixer bowl on medium speed until creamy, about 30 seconds. Add both sugars; beat on medium speed for 2 minutes. Scrape down bowl, add egg and vanilla; beat well. Beat in puree (mixture will look slightly curdled). Add dry mixture and blend on low speed until well-blended.

Using a small scoop, portion dough and place onto sheet pans, leaving about 1 inch between for spreading. Bake 13 to 15 minutes or until light golden brown and firm to the touch. Cool cookies completely before filling.

Prepare frosting:
Beat butter in electric mixer bowl on medium speed for 1 minute. Add confectioners' sugar and continue beating on medium speed for 2 minutes. Turn off mixer and add marshmallow, vanilla and salt; beat on low speed until well-blended. Place half of the cookies upside down on parchment paper. Pipe or spread frosting onto cookies. Top with remaining cookies and press down to create a sandwich. Keep filled cookies in an airtight container for up to 3 days.

Makes about (20) 2-inch cookies.

Pumpkin Crumble Bars

Pumpkin Crumble Bars

I was inspired to create these bars by a couple of recipes in my files. The orange zest pairs well with the pumpkin and cinnamon, but can be eliminated if desired.

1½ cups all-purpose flour
1 cup dark brown sugar
1 tsp. baking powder
½ tsp. salt
6 ounces (1½ sticks) cold butter, cut into pieces
1 cup old-fashioned oats
1 cup pumpkin puree
1 can (14 ounce) sweetened condensed milk
1 tsp. ground cinnamon
1 tbsp. finely grated orange zest (1 orange)

Preheat oven to 350°F. Spray a 13x9x2-inch baking pan with nonstick spray.

Place flour, brown sugar, baking powder and salt in food processor; pulse several times to combine. Add butter; pulse several times until butter is in small pieces. Add oats and pulse to combine. Measure out 2½ cups and press evenly into bottom of prepared pan. Set aside remaining crumble.

Whisk together pumpkin puree, milk, cinnamon and zest in medium bowl. Pour over bottom crust. Gently sprinkle remaining crumble over filling; press down evenly.

Bake 40 to 42 minutes or until golden brown and filling appears set. Cool bars completely before cutting. Dust bars with confectioners' sugar if desired. Keep bars covered at room temperature up to 5 days or freeze for longer storage.

Makes 24 bars.

Pumpkin Caramel
Cheesecake
(p. 44)

Frozen Chocolate
Beet Mousse Pie
(p. 61)

Sweet Potato Swirl
Cheesecake
(p. 50)

Custards
& Mousses

Avocado Chocolate Mousse

The creaminess of avocado creates a spectacular backdrop to the cocoa and frankly, you will never know the avocado is there. Be sure to try this mousse in a variety of ways noted below.

4 ripe avocados
⅔ cup unsweetened cocoa powder
½ cup honey
2 tbsp. vanilla extract
¼ tsp. salt
2 containers (8 ounce each) frozen whipped topping, thawed

Cut and remove flesh of avocados; place into food processor bowl. Add cocoa powder, honey, vanilla and salt. Pulse to combine well and puree avocados; scrape down bowl as needed. Puree until smooth. Transfer to medium bowl and fold in (1) whipped topping container.

When ready to serve, garnish with additional whipped topping.

Makes about 6 cups mousse.

Mousse Cups:
Fill glass dishes with mousse, garnish with fresh fruit and additional whipped topping if desired.

Double Chocolate Mousse Cups:
Fill edible chocolate dessert cups with mousse and fresh fruit as desired (see photo opposite).

Frozen Mousse Pie:
Fill a 9-inch chocolate crumb crust with mousse and freeze at least two hours. Garnish with additional whipped topping and cut into 8 servings. Serve slightly frozen; it will taste like ice cream!

Double Chocolate
Mousse Cups

Pumpkin Caramel Cheesecake

This yummy cheesecake uses a premade crust and a simple filling. You don't have to wait long to eat this cheesecake as it bakes within 45 minutes and cools within three hours.

1 pkg. (8 ounce) cream cheese, softened
½ cup dark brown sugar, packed
2 eggs
1 tsp. vanilla extract
⅔ cup pumpkin puree
½ tsp. pumpkin pie spice
¼ cup heavy cream
Pinch salt
1 (9-inch) graham cracker crust
Caramel topping
Whipped topping
Roasted pumpkin seeds

Preheat oven to 325°F.

Beat cream cheese and brown sugar in electric mixer bowl on medium-low speed 2 to 3 minutes or until mixture is smooth and free of lumps. Add eggs, one at a time, mixing well after each. Add puree, spice, cream, and salt. Mix on low until well-blended. Pour batter into crust. Bake 35 to 40 minutes or until cheesecake is mostly firm when pan is shaken.

Cool at room temperature 20 minutes, then refrigerate at least 2 to 3 hours.

To serve, drizzle with caramel, top with whipped topping and sprinkle with pumpkin seeds. Keep covered and refrigerated up to 4 days.

Makes 8 servings.

Tip: For a crispy crust, follow package directions to bake crust.

Pumpkin Cranberry Bread Pudding

Bread pudding is always a great way to use up not-so-fresh bread. Raisins can be used instead of cranberries.

7 to 8 slices cinnamon swirl bread, about ½ of a 1-pound loaf
⅓ cup dried cranberries
3 eggs
1½ cups warm milk
¾ cup pumpkin puree
½ cup light brown sugar
2 tbsp. butter, melted
1 tsp. vanilla extract
¼ tsp. pumpkin pie spice
Pinch salt

Cut bread slices into bite-sized pieces (do not remove crust) and place into medium bowl. Toss in cranberries.

Whisk together eggs in large bowl. Whisk in milk, pumpkin, sugar, butter, vanilla, spice, and salt. Add bread and cranberries into custard; stir well to make sure all bread is covered with custard. Let stand 10 minutes, stirring once.

Preheat oven to 350°F. Have ready a 9-inch square baking dish and a larger roasting pan for a water bath.

Pour bread mixture into baking dish and place in larger roasting pan. Place into preheated oven and pour hot water into roasting pan halfway up side of baking dish. Bake until pudding reaches 175°F or custard is firm throughout, about 40 to 45 minutes. Cover dish with foil during baking if bread on top starts to overbrown.

Cool 10 minutes before serving warm or serve well-chilled. Tastes great drizzled with caramel sauce or maple syrup. Refrigerate covered pudding for up to three days.

Makes 9 servings.

Roasted Red Pepper
Cheesecake

Roasted Red Pepper Cheesecake

You have probably never eaten a savory cheesecake, but this one takes the cake! Serve it right from the baking dish at your next party or brunch and watch it disappear!

2 pkgs. (8 ounce each) cream cheese, softened
1 shallot, finely chopped
1 tbsp. garlic paste
2 eggs
½ cup sour cream
½ cup heavy cream
4 ounces grated Cheddar cheese, about 1 cup
½ cup chopped, jarred roasted red peppers
½ tsp. salt

Preheat oven to 325°F. Have ready a 9x2-inch decorative ceramic baking dish.

Beat cream cheese in electric mixer on medium speed for two minutes or until smooth. Add shallot and garlic paste; beat until well-blended. Add eggs, one at a time, beating well after each. Scrape down bowl and add sour cream; beat on low until well-blended. On low speed, gradually add heavy cream. Scrape down bowl; add cheese, peppers and salt on low speed.

Pour batter into baking dish. Bake 45 to 50 minutes or until firm. Cool at least one hour at room temperature, then refrigerate until well-chilled, about four hours.

Serve with crispy toasted baguette slices, crackers or tortilla chips as an appetizer. Keep covered and refrigerated for 3 days.

Makes 1 cheesecake.

Rutabaga Bread Pudding

I have never paired rutabaga with bread pudding until now! I was surprised at how good this vegetable translated into a dessert.

7 to 8 slices cinnamon swirl bread, about ½ 1-pound loaf
1 cup diced canned rutabaga, drained
3 eggs
2 cups warm milk
¾ cup light brown sugar
2 tbsp. butter, melted
1 tsp. ground cinnamon
1 tsp. vanilla extract
¼ tsp. salt

Preheat oven to 350°F. Have ready a 9-inch baking dish and a larger roasting pan for a water bath.

Cut bread slices into bite-sized pieces (do not remove crust) and place in large bowl. Place rutabaga pieces on top; set aside.

Whisk together eggs in medium bowl. Whisk in milk, sugar, butter, cinnamon, vanilla and salt. Pour over bread and rutabaga; stir to combine well, making sure all the bread is covered with the custard. Let stand about 10 minutes, stirring once.

Pour bread mixture into baking dish and place in larger roasting pan. Place into preheated oven and pour hot water into roasting pan halfway up side of baking dish. Bake until pudding reaches 175°F or custard is firm throughout, about 40 to 45 minutes. Cover dish with foil during baking if bread on top starts to overbrown.

Cool 10 minutes before serving warm or serve well-chilled. Tastes great drizzled with caramel sauce or maple syrup. Refrigerate covered pudding for up to three days.

Makes 9 servings.

Savory Vegetable Bread Pudding

This is a great way to use up older loaves of bread, as well as leftover cooked or raw vegetables. I tested the recipe with both Focaccia (p. 74) and Tomato Herb Bread (p. 83). I used zucchini, roasted red peppers, and shallots, but most cooked vegetables will work, such as mushrooms, asparagus, broccoli, or cauliflower. It's important not to add too many vegetables or the custard may not set properly.

1 tbsp. olive oil
1 tbsp. butter
1 small zucchini, diced
1 small shallot, finely diced
¼ cup chopped jarred roasted red peppers
6 eggs
3 cups warm milk
Parmesan cheese, optional
Salt and pepper to taste
4 cups bread cubes

Preheat oven to 350°F. Have ready (4) 2-cup ramekins or an 8 to 10 cup baking dish.

Heat oil and butter in medium sauté pan on medium heat. Add zucchini and shallots. Stir and cook for 3 to 4 minutes or until zucchini begins to soften. Add peppers and continue to cook an additional minute. Remove vegetables from pan to cool; set aside.

Whisk together eggs in large bowl. Whisk in milk while whisking constantly. Add Parmesan as desired, as well as salt and pepper. Add bread cubes and vegetables. Stir to coat bread well with custard. Let stand 5 to 10 minutes, stirring once.

If using ramekins, divide mixture between cups and place cups in large roasting pan. Or pour mixture into large baking dish and place in large roasting pan. Place roasting pan in oven and add hot water, coming up halfway to dishes.

Bake ramekins for 50 to 55 minutes or large baking dish 45 to 50 minutes, or until internal temperature in the middle reaches 175°F.

Remove baking dishes from roasting pan and cool 10 to 15 minutes before serving warm. Leftovers can be covered and refrigerated up to 2 days.

Makes 4 to 6 servings.

Tip: If using raw vegetables, make sure to sauté and cook well. If using all pre-cooked vegetables, the cooking step can be eliminated.

Sweet Potato Swirl Cheesecake

I prefer making cheesecakes in prepared crusts; they are easier to make, they have a shorter bake time and the cheesecake cools faster, so you can devour it quicker!

½ cup sweet potato puree
½ tsp. ground cinnamon
1 egg yolk
1 pkg. (8 ounce) cream cheese, softened
½ cup granulated sugar
1 egg
1 tsp. vanilla extract
¼ cup sour cream
¼ cup heavy cream
1 (9-inch) graham cracker or shortbread crust

Preheat oven to 325°F.

Stir together the potato puree, cinnamon and yolk in small bowl; set aside.

Beat cream cheese and sugar in electric mixer bowl on medium speed about 2 minutes or until no cheese lumps remain. Scrape down bowl and paddle. On medium speed, add egg and vanilla; blend well. Add sour cream and heavy cream; mix on low just until combined. Remove 1/3 cup batter and stir into puree/cinnamon mixture to mix well.

Spoon dollops of both cheesecake batter and sweet potato/cinnamon batter into prepared crust. Using a toothpick, swirl the dollops to create a marble pattern, being careful not to pull toothpick though bottom crust.

Bake 35 to 40 minutes or until mostly set when jiggled, but not browned. Let cool 30 minutes, then refrigerate at least 2 hours before serving.

Keep covered in refrigerator for up to four days.

Makes 8 servings.

Tip: For a crispy crust, follow package directions to bake crust.

Veggie Mousses

These mousses begin with instant pudding, a vegetable puree and whipped topping. Try one—or all three!

Basic Mousse:
1 pkg. (3.4 ounce) instant vanilla pudding
1½ cups cold milk
1 container (8 ounce) frozen whipped topping, thawed, divided

Whisk together pudding mix and cold milk in medium bowl for 2 minutes; then refrigerate 5 minutes.

Pumpkin Maple Mousse:
¾ cup pumpkin puree
¼ tsp. pumpkin pie spice
½ tsp. maple extract

Whisk the puree, spice and maple into the chilled pudding mixture. Fold in half of the whipped topping. Serve with the additional whipped topping.

Sweet Potato Mousse:
¾ cup sweet potato puree
¼ tsp. ground cinnamon
Pinch nutmeg

Whisk the puree, cinnamon and nutmeg into the chilled pudding mixture. Fold in half of the whipped topping. Serve with additional whipped topping.

Carrot Ginger Orange Mousse:
1 jar (4 ounce) carrot baby food, about ⅓ cup
Pinch ground ginger
1 tsp. finely grated orange zest (about ½ orange)

Whisk the carrot, ginger and zest into the chilled pudding mixture. Fold in half of the whipped topping. Serve with additional whipped topping.

Each mousse serves 6 to 8.

Tip: For ideas on how to use these mousses in more unique pastries, check out the Veggie Mousse Trifle on page 60 or the Veggie Mousse Eclairs on page 59.

Carrot Cake Mousse Trifle
(p. 60)

Pastries

Chocolate Beet
Walnut Tart
(recipe opposite)

Chocolate Beet Walnut Tart

Beets and chocolate are a natural pairing. When the tart is cut, you can see a thin streak of red between the filling and crust.

Crust:
1 cup all-purpose flour
½ cup walnuts
¼ pound (1 stick) cold butter, cut into pieces
¼ cup confectioners' sugar
¼ tsp. salt

Filling:
½ cup heavy cream
½ cup 100% beet juice (no additional ingredients)
¼ cup sour cream
¼ cup granulated sugar
Pinch salt
8 ounces high-quality semisweet chocolate, chopped

One container (8 ounce) frozen whipped topping, thawed
Dried beet chips, chocolate shavings, decorations or mini chocolate chips

Prepare Crust:
Have ready a 9x1-inch round or 14x4½-inch rectangular non-stick tart pan with a removable bottom.

Place all ingredients into food processor and pulse until walnuts are finely chopped and butter is in small pieces. Place crust into tart pan and press down evenly on bottom of pan and press crust onto sides. Cover and refrigerate at least 1 hour or overnight.

Preheat oven to 375°F. Place tart pan onto sheet pan and bake 25 to 30 minutes or until golden brown. Remove from oven to cool.

Prepare Filling:
Place heavy cream, beet juice, sour cream, sugar and salt in medium saucepan over medium heat. Whisk to combine, heating just until bubbles start to form around edge of pan (do not boil). Turn off heat and add chopped chocolate. Stir until chocolate melts and mixture is smooth. Pour into cooled crust. Refrigerate at least 2 hours, covering with plastic wrap once filling is firm.

When ready to serve, decorate tart with whipped topping, beet chips, and chocolate decorations. Let tart stand at room temperature 10 minutes before cutting into 12 servings (the chocolate filling has a better flavor at room temperature). Keep covered and refrigerated up to three days.

Makes 12 servings.

Rhubarb Mixed Berry Crisps

Rhubarb is very seasonal (April through June) and can be hard to find frozen in off season, so enjoy while you can!

1 pkg. (16 ounce) frozen sliced rhubarb, or fresh rhubarb, sliced to measure 4 cups
1 pkg. (10 ounce) frozen mixed berries
2 tsp. fresh lemon juice
1 cup granulated sugar
3 tbsp. cornstarch
½ tsp. ground ginger
1 recipe Streusel Topping (page 17)

Preheat oven to 375°F. Have ready (4) large individual baking dishes or (1) 9-inch glass or ceramic baking dish (do not use a metal pan as the lemon juice with react with the metal).

Place rhubarb and berries in a medium bowl. Add lemon juice, sugar, cornstarch and ginger; toss to coat fruit well. Divide fruit among dishes. Place dishes on sheet pan covered with parchment paper (to catch fruit drippings). Bake 15 minutes.

Meanwhile, prepare Streusel Topping. Remove pan from oven and divide the topping among the dishes. Place back into oven and bake 30 minutes or until fruit mixture is bubbling around edges.

Cool 15 minutes before serving. Top with vanilla ice cream if desired.

Makes 4 servings.

Roasted Rhubarb and Strawberry Shortcakes

I was inspired to roast the fruit by "Bake" magazine. You will not believe how roasting intensifies the flavors of both the rhubarb and strawberries, making these shortcakes extraordinary!

24 ounces fresh or frozen (thawed) rhubarb slices, about 6 cups
1 cup granulated sugar
2 tsp. fresh lemon juice
Pinch sea salt
2 pounds, stemmed, sliced fresh strawberries
1 cup granulated sugar
2 tsp. fresh lemon juice
Pinch sea salt
1 baked pound cake or cake dessert shells
Whipped topping, as desired

Preheat oven to 400°F. Line (2) large sheet pans with foil.

Place rhubarb, 1 cup sugar and 2 tsp. lemon juice in large bowl; stir to mix well. Let stand to exude juice while roasting strawberries.

Place strawberries, 1 cup sugar, and 2 tsp. lemon juice in large bowl; stir to mix well. Spread berries onto sheet pan and sprinkle with salt. Roast in oven 20 to 22 minutes, stirring halfway through. Remove from oven and cool. Repeat the same roasting procedure and cooking time with the rhubarb. Let cool completely.

Combine cooled strawberries and rhubarb in large bowl. Cover and refrigerate until ready to use. Keeps five days.

To assemble shortcakes, slice pound cake into 8 slices. Place on individual dessert plates or glass dishes. Top with roasted fruit (include some of the yummy juice) and finish with whipped topping.

Makes 8 shortcakes.

Variation: The roasted fruit also tastes great on top of ice cream or on top of a sweet scone!

Sweet Potato Brown Butter Pie

This recipe is a great way to use convenient canned yams and enjoy this pie any time of the year. The browned butter with the orange zest is a delicious combination of flavors. Try making a simple pie dough on page 15. Or use a pre-made pie crust. Do not skip the par-baking of the crust; the crust on the bottom of the pie needs to be partially baked.

1 (9-inch) unbaked, chilled pie crust
Pie weights*
4 tbsp. (½ stick) butter
1 can (15 ounce) sweet potatoes/yams in syrup
2 eggs
½ cup dark brown sugar

½ cup granulated sugar
½ cup heavy cream
1 tsp. vanilla extract
½ tsp. ground cinnamon
½ tsp. salt
1 tbsp. finely grated orange zest

Preheat oven to 400°F.

To par-bake pie crust, line crust with foil and weigh down with desired pie weights. Bake in oven 15 minutes or crust begins to brown. Remove foil with weights and continue to bake another 5 to 7 minutes or until crust is light brown. Remove from oven; reduce oven to 350°F.

To brown butter, place butter in small saucepan over medium-low heat. Let butter melt and continue to stir and heat until butter starts to sizzle and begins to brown. Pour very hot butter into heatproof dish to cool; set aside.

Drain potatoes from syrup, reserving about ¼ cup syrup. Place potatoes and ¼ cup syrup in medium bowl and mash, using a potato masher or fork. Whisk in eggs, both sugars, cream, vanilla, cinnamon, salt and orange zest. Whisk in cooled brown butter. Pour custard into prepared crust.

Bake pie 38 to 40 minutes or until middle of pie is just about set. Cover edges of crust during baking to overbrowning. Cool pie 1 hour before serving or refrigerate. Keep pie covered and refrigerated up to three days.

Serve with whipped topping or ice cream.

Makes 8 servings.

Tip: The easiest and cheapest pie weights are dried beans. Purchase 2 bags black and/or pinto beans and re-use them only for par-baking pie crusts or tart shells. Once cooled, store them in a resealable plastic bag in the pantry.

Veggie Mousse Éclairs

Here are some ideas to transform an ordinary éclair into an extraordinary one! Change up the filling by using Avocado Chocolate Mousse, Chocolate Beet Mousse, Sweet Potato Pudding, or Pumpkin Maple Mousse. Top them all with the same chocolate glaze; yummy!

1 batch Éclairs (see recipe on page 14)
½ batch Chocolate Glaze (see recipe on page 12)
Medium star tip
Large decorating bag

Prepare éclairs and desired filling separately; cool completely.

Before assembling éclairs, prepare ½ batch Chocolate Glaze; set aside in small, wide, microwaveable bowl.

To assemble éclairs, turn all éclairs upside down on large sheet pan that is lined with parchment paper. Using the star tip, make a hole in the middle bottom of each éclair. Insert star tip into decorating bag and fill with mousse/pudding. Insert star tip into holes in éclairs, squeezing filling into one end, then turn bag to fill other end of éclair. Refill decorating bag as needed.

Once all éclairs are filled, dip the tops into chocolate glaze, turn over and place onto sheet pan. Keep éclairs covered and refrigerated until ready to serve. Best if eaten within three days.

Makes (24) 3-inch éclairs.

Avocado Chocolate Mousse:
Prepare the recipe on page 42 and fill éclairs as noted above. Top chocolate glaze with just a couple sprinkles of coarse sea salt.

Chocolate Beet Mousse:
Prepare the recipe on page 61 and fill éclairs as noted above. Top chocolate glaze with toasted, chopped walnuts.

Sweet Potato Mousse:
Prepare the recipe on page 51 and fill éclairs as noted above. Top chocolate glaze with toffee bits.

Pumpkin Maple Mousse:
Prepare the recipe on page 51 and fill éclairs as noted above. Top chocolate glaze with toasted, chopped pecans.

Veggie Mousse Trifle

A trifle is a layered dessert, consisting of a custard, cake, whipped topping and any other crunchy foods (nuts, seeds, coconut, etc.). It's usually served in a tall glass dish to display the layers. Try a trifle with any of the veggie mousses in this book. Use a cake flavor that compliments the mousse.

1 small baked cake or brownies, cut into bite-sized pieces
2 batches any desired flavor of Veggie Mousse, page 51
2 containers (8 ounce each) frozen whipped topping, thawed

Have ready a large glass trifle dish. To assemble trifle, layer the cake, mousse, whipped topping and if desired, a crunchy food. Repeat the layers to fill the dish. Top with whipped topping and decorate as desired. Cover and refrigerate up to 3 days; serve well-chilled.

Serves 12 to 16.

Variations:

Pumpkin Maple Mousse or Sweet Potato Mousse Trifle: Use a spice or cinnamon swirl cake and add chopped pecans or honey-roasted pumpkin seeds for crunch. Drizzle caramel topping on top for added flavor.

Pumpkin Mousse Butterscotch Trifle: For the Pumpkin Maple Mousse, eliminate the maple extract. Bake and cool a batch of the Pumpkin Butterscotch Brownies on page 36. Use chopped pecans or additional butterscotch chips for crunch. Drizzle with butterscotch topping for added flavor.

Carrot Ginger Orange Mousse Trifle: Use a spice or carrot cake and add chopped walnuts or dried cranberries/raisins for crunch. Top dish with Candied Carrot Curls and Candied Walnuts (see page 16 for recipe).

Frozen Chocolate Beet Mousse Pie

No one will ever know that beet juice is an ingredient in this ice cream-like frozen dessert.

1 (9-inch) dark chocolate cookie crumb crust
½ cup heavy cream
½ cup 100% beet juice (no additional ingredients)
¼ cup sour cream
¼ cup granulated sugar
6 ounces high-quality semisweet chocolate, finely chopped
2 containers (8 ounce each) frozen whipped topping, thawed, divided

Follow crumb crust package directions to prepare for a baked crust; set aside to cool.

Combine cream, beet juice, sour cream and sugar in small saucepan and heat over medium low heat. Once small bubbles appear on outer edges, turn off heat. Add chopped chocolate and stir to combine and chocolate completely melts. Pour mixture into medium bowl and cool for 15 minutes. Meanwhile, remove one whipped topping container from refrigerator. Fold together chocolate/beet mixture and one container of whipped topping. Spoon mixture into prepared crumb crust, cover and place in freezer for at least 2 hours.

When ready to serve, let pie sit at room temperature for 10 minutes. Cut into 8 pieces and top with additional whipped topping.

Makes 8 servings.

Beet Walnut
Ginger Bread
(p. 64)

Sweet Potato Herb Drop
Biscuit (p. 70)

Roasted Poblano Pepper
& Corn Muffins (p. 68)

Quick Breads

Beet Walnut Ginger Bread

This beautiful bread has an earthy flavor, accented with ginger and walnuts. Use baby beets, which are slightly sweeter than fully grown beets.

1 cup all-purpose flour
½ cup whole wheat flour
½ cup granulated sugar
½ cup light brown sugar
1 tsp. baking powder
1 tsp. baking soda
1 tsp. salt
½ tsp. ground ginger
½ cup chopped walnuts

3 eggs
1 pkg. (8 ounce) peeled and steamed baby beets, pureed with 1 tbsp. water
1 container (5.3 ounce) plain Greek yogurt
½ cup light olive oil
1 tsp. vanilla extract
2 cups confectioners' sugar
¼ cup beet juice

Preheat oven to 350°F. Spray a 9x5-inch loaf pan with nonstick spray and line bottom with parchment paper.

Stir together both flours, both sugars, baking powder, baking soda, salt, ginger and walnuts in medium bowl; set aside.

Whisk together the eggs in large bowl. Whisk in beet puree, yogurt, oil and vanilla. Stir in flour mixture just until combined; do not overmix. Pour batter into prepared pan and bake 50 to 55 minutes or until toothpick inserted into center comes out clean.

Cool bread in pan 10 minutes, then invert onto cooling rack. Whisk together confectioners' sugar and beet juice and drizzle over warm bread. Let cool completely before serving. Keep bread covered in an airtight container for up to five days.

Makes 1 loaf.

Loaf pictured on page 62 can also be baked in an 11x4½-inch pan, purchased at IKEA.

Carrot Cake Waffles

What a great way to add vegetables to breakfast! Use a Belgium waffle mix, which makes preparation fast and easy. Make sure the carrots are finely grated for fast cooking.

1½ cups waffle Mix
½ tsp. ground cinnamon
½ cup finely shredded carrots
¼ cup raisins
1 egg
⅔ cup cold water
3 tbsp. vegetable or corn oil

Mix together waffle mix, cinnamon, carrots, and raisins in small bowl.

Whisk together the egg, water and oil. Add dry/carrot mix and stir until just combined (do not overmix). Let mixture stand 2 minutes before cooking.

Heat waffle iron and cook waffles according to manufacturer's directions.

Serve immediately with maple syrup.

Makes 3 large round waffles.

Corn & Cheese Corn Bread

Cornbread mixes are convenient to use. Spruce it up with corn, cheese and roasted red peppers, which not only add flavor, but great texture.

1 box (15 ounce) Honey Cornbread mix, plus ingredients to prepare mix
1 cup grated sharp Cheddar cheese
½ cup frozen corn kernels
½ cup finely chopped roasted red pepper or drained canned chilies, optional

Preheat oven to 400°F. Spray a 9-inch square baking pan with non-stick spray; set aside.

Prepare cornbread mix following package directions, adding cheese, corn and peppers if desired. Pour into prepared pan and bake 24 to 26 minutes or until golden brown and center of cornbread is firm to the touch. Let cool 10 minutes before serving warm. Keep leftover cornbread in an airtight container.

Makes 9 servings.

Onion & Mustard Drop Biscuits

These flavorful biscuits are quick to prepare and go well with a variety of meals.

2 cups all-purpose flour
1 tbsp. baking powder
1 tsp. salt
½ cup chopped yellow or sweet white onion
1 tbsp. chopped fresh dill (or 1 tsp. dried dill)
4 tbsp. (½ stick) butter, cold and cut into pieces
1 cup cold milk
¼ cup Dijon mustard

Preheat oven to 400°F. Line a large sheet pan with parchment paper.

Place flour, baking powder, salt, onion, and dill in food processor. Pulse 3 to 4 times to blend. Add butter and pulse another 3 to 4 times to cut butter and into small pieces.

In medium bowl, whisk together milk and mustard. Add flour/butter mixture and stir just until mixture comes together. Using a scoop, portion biscuits onto prepared pan.

Bake 15 to 17 minutes or until lightly browned and firm. Let stand 5 minutes before serving warm. Store leftover biscuits in airtight container.

Makes 9 to 10 biscuits.

Pumpkin Apple Pancakes

These pancakes are not only yummy, but have fruit and vegetables to boot! Apples add a nice texture. Don't have any apples? Replace with dried fruit, such as cranberries or raisins.

2 cups all-purpose flour
4 tbsp. granulated sugar
2 tsp. baking powder
1 tsp. baking soda
1 tsp. pumpkin pie spice
½ tsp. salt
1 small apple, peeled, cored and grated (Gala or Honeycrisp)
1 egg
1¾ cup cold milk
1 cup pumpkin puree
2 tbsp. vegetable oil
1 tsp. vanilla extract

Preheat griddle.

Whisk together flour, sugar, baking powder, baking soda, spice, and salt in small bowl. Stir in grated apples; set aside.

In large bowl, whisk the egg. Whisk in milk, pumpkin, oil and vanilla. Whisk in dry mixture JUST until mixed. Do not overmix. Let stand 1 to 2 minutes.

Lightly grease griddle and ladle out pancake batter. Cook 2 minutes or until top is very bubbly. Turn over pancakes and cook about 1 to 1½ minutes. Remove from griddle onto large plate and cover with foil to keep warm.

Serve warm with maple syrup or any desired syrup.

Makes about (14) 3-inch pancakes.

Roasted Poblano Pepper & Corn Muffins

Roasting the poblano pepper takes about 45 minutes to prepare, but adds a wonderful flavor to these homemade muffins.

1 large poblano pepper
Olive oil
1 cup frozen corn kernels
2 tbsp. finely chopped onion
1 cup all-purpose flour
¾ cup yellow cornmeal, plus extra for dusting pan
2 tsp. baking powder
1½ tsp. salt
½ tsp. baking soda
2 eggs
1 cup sour cream
¼ cup honey
4 tbsp. (½ stick) butter, melted

Preheat oven to 425°F. Line a small pan with foil. Coat pepper with oil and place on foil-lined pan. Roast in oven for 30 minutes, turning pepper 3 to 4 times with tongs to evenly roast. Remove from oven and place pepper in small bowl; cover with plastic wrap and let stand 15 minutes. Reduce oven temperature to 400°F. Spray a 12-cup muffin pan with nonstick spray and sprinkle cups with cornmeal.

Remove pepper from bowl and gently peel to remove charred skin. Place on cutting board, cut in half and remove stem and seeds. Finely chop pepper, place back into small bowl and add corn and onions; set aside.

Combine flour, cornmeal, baking powder, salt and baking soda in small bowl; set aside.

Whisk eggs together in medium bowl. Whisk in sour cream, honey and butter. Fold in flour/cornmeal mixture and vegetable mixture. Mix just until combined; do not overmix.

Scoop batter evenly between muffin cups. Bake 15 to 17 minutes or until golden brown and muffin tops are firm to the touch. Remove from oven and let cool in pan 5 minutes. Invert pan to remove muffins onto cooling rack. Serve warm or cool completely and store in an airtight container.

Makes 12 muffins.

Sweet Potato Date Nut Muffins

These moist muffins are a great use of some leftover cooked sweet potatoes. The dates can be replaced with dried fruit, such as cranberries or raisins.

1½ cups all-purpose flour
½ cup granulated sugar
1 tbsp. baking powder
1 tsp. pumpkin pie spice
½ tsp. salt
2 eggs
⅔ cup sweet potato puree
½ cup milk
¼ cup light olive oil
1 tsp. vanilla extract
⅓ cup diced dates
⅓ cup chopped walnuts

Preheat oven to 375°F. Line 12 muffin cups with paper liners; set aside.

Whisk together the flour, sugar, baking powder, spice and salt in small bowl; set aside.

Whisk together the eggs in medium bowl. Whisk in puree, milk, oil and vanilla. Stir in flour mixture, dates and walnuts; mix briefly. Do not overmix.

Scoop batter into muffin cups (cups will be ¾ full). Bake 18 to 20 minutes or until firm to the touch or a toothpick inserted into center comes out clean. Cool muffins in pan 5 minutes, then invert to remove muffins. Serve warm or store in an airtight container for up to three days.

Makes 12 muffins.

Tip: Purchase pre-chopped dates in packages that are coated in oat flour to prevent stickiness.

Sweet Potato Herb Drop Biscuit

These savory biscuits are a great side for a ham or pork dinner. The dried sage can be replaced with most any dried herbs; the sage reminds me of Thanksgiving time.

1¼ cups all-purpose flour
1½ tsp. baking powder
1 tsp. salt
1 tbsp. finely chopped shallots or yellow onion
½ tsp. dried ground sage
4 tbsp. (½ stick) butter, cold and cut into pieces
½ cup cold milk
½ cup cold sweet potato puree
2 tbsp. butter, melted

Preheat oven to 375°F. Line sheet pan with parchment paper.

In food processor bowl, combine flour, baking powder, salt, shallots and sage. Add butter and pulse several times to cut butter into small pieces, about the size of peas.

In medium bowl, whisk together milk and puree. Add flour/butter mixture on top. Stir together until just mixed and all flour is absorbed (dough will be thick). Scoop dough into 8 mounds onto prepared sheet pans.

Bake 15 to 17 minutes or until lightly browned and top of biscuits are firm. Drizzle melted butter over biscuits; let cool 5 minutes before serving. Store leftover biscuits in airtight container.

Makes 8 biscuits.

Zucchini Bread

I have made this bread throughout my pastry career, especially at various caterers. It's a wonderful addition to a breakfast tray.

2 cups all-purpose flour
2 tsp. ground cinnamon
1½ tsp. baking powder
1 tsp. salt
½ tsp. baking soda
2 cups grated zucchini (about 2 medium)
½ cup chopped walnuts
3 eggs
½ cup granulated sugar
½ cup light brown sugar
⅔ cup light olive oil or vegetable oil
2 tsp. vanilla extract

Preheat oven to 350°F. Spray a 9x5-inch loaf pan with nonstick spray and line bottom of pan with parchment paper.

Combine flour, cinnamon, baking powder, salt and baking soda in medium bowl. Add zucchini and walnuts; toss to mix; set aside.

Whisk together eggs in large bowl. Whisk in both sugars, oil and vanilla. Pour flour/zucchini mixture on top and mix together with spatula until well-blended (mixture will be thick). Scrape batter into prepared pan. Bake 60-65 minutes or until toothpick inserted into center comes out clean. Cool in pan 10 minutes, then invert to remove bread. Cool completely before serving. Store bread in airtight container at room temperature for up to 3 days.

Makes 1 loaf.

Variation: Replace grated zucchini with grated carrots or do a combination, using 1 cup of each vegetable. This loaf can also be baked in an 11x4½-inch pan, purchased at IKEA.

Pumpkin Cinnamon Pecan
Ring (p. 78)

Caramelized Onion
Focaccia
(p. 74)

Spinach Potato Bread
(p. 81)

Tomato Herb Rolls
(p. 83)

Yeast Breads

Caramelized Onion Focaccia

I have made this bread for so many catered events I have lost count. But, it's so good that I never tire of making it, especially on a cold, winter day. My version includes infusing fresh rosemary into the water for the bread, which gives the bread a wonderful flavor! This recipe makes one large sheet pan, which is thick enough to be cut in half to fill with meats and cheeses for a yummy sandwich!

3 tbsp. finely chopped fresh rosemary, about 3 to 4 sprigs
2 cups boiling water

Combine rosemary and boiling water in bowl; let sit 30 minutes to 45 minutes. Strain rosemary and pour infused warm water into mixer bowl; set aside drained rosemary for later use.

Bread:
1 pkg. (¼ ounce) instant yeast (about 2¼ teaspoons)
3 tbsp. olive oil
2 tbsp. drained rosemary
6 cups bread or "00" flour
1 tbsp. salt

Glaze:
2 tbsp. olive oil
1 egg
Olive oil

Topping:
1 large yellow or white sweet onion, peeled and thinly sliced into rings
2 tbsp. olive oil
2 tbsp. butter
1 tsp. salt
¼ cup finely grated or shredded Parmesan or Romano cheese
Coarse sea salt
1 tbsp. drained rosemary

Preheat oven to 250°F. The stovetop will be a warm place to let the dough rise.

Dough:
Add yeast, 3 tbsp. olive oil, 2 tbsp. rosemary, bread flour, and salt to mixer bowl with rosemary water. Beat with paddle attachment until a soft dough forms and cleans the bowl. If dough sticks to sides of bowl, add a little bread flour. This dough is meant to be a little moist and sticky. Continue mixing for 5 to 6 minutes on low speed to develop the gluten.

Spray a large bowl with nonstick spray and place dough in bowl and cover loosely with plastic wrap. Place on warm stovetop for about 1 hour or until dough is doubled in size.

Topping:
While dough is rising, prepare the caramelized onions. Place 2 tbsp. olive oil and butter into large sauté pan; heat on medium for 2 to 3 minutes. Add onions and salt; cook and stir until onions are soft and translucent, about 5 to 6 minutes. Remove onions from pan to cool; set aside.

When dough is ready, remove from bowl and place onto a lightly floured surface. Punch down dough to remove excess gas. Stretch and shape dough into a large ball; cover with plastic wrap and let rest 10 to 15 minutes. This step will make the final shaping much easier. Turn off oven and place large, deep roasting pan in bottom of oven.

Glaze:
Prepare the glaze by whisking together the 2 tbsp. olive oil and egg in small bowl; set aside. Brush a 17x12-inch rimmed sheet pan with about 2 tbsp. olive oil, making sure to coat the rimmed edges as well.

Place dough ball in center of prepared pan and with oiled hands, press dough down, stretching and pressing to fill pan (dough will fill about ¾ of the pan and will expand more when baked). Brush top of dough with glaze and place sheet pan into warm oven (make sure oven is not hotter than 120°F or the yeast might become inactive). Fill the empty roasting pan with hot water (adds humidity to oven). Close oven and let dough rise 20 to 25 minutes. Remove dough from oven; remove roasting pan with water from oven as well.

Preheat oven to 400°F. Sprinkle Parmesan, salt and remaining drained Rosemary on top of bread. Toss cooled onions with about 1 tbsp. olive oil (this keeps onions from burning during baking). Gently lay onions on top, careful not to press down to deflate bread. Bake 30 to 35 minutes or until internal temperature reaches 195°F in the center. Immediately remove bread from hot pan, using a large pancake spatula to get underneath bread. Cool bread on cooling rack at least 10 minutes before slicing.

Store bread in airtight container for up to two days. Freeze for longer storage.

Makes 1 large sheet.

Tip: "00" flour is a finely ground, low protein specialty flour found in 2 pound bags. I find it in the Italian section of the supermarket or ethnic stores. This flour is great for pasta, pizza or Focaccia.

Variation: If you prefer a flatter Focaccia, divide the dough in half before shaping and divide between (2) large sheet pans.

Cauliflower Cheese Bread

Thanks to frozen, mashed cauliflower, this bread comes together quickly and along with the Parmesan cheese, is a soft, flavorful bread. You can use plain mashed cauliflower or use one with cheese or herbs included; they all work fine. And forget about multiple steps for shaping the bread. Simply place in the loaf pan, cover and let rise in a warm place for 90 minutes.

1½ cups cooked, mashed cauliflower (with olive oil and sea salt)
1½ cups warm milk
1 pkg. (¼ ounce) instant yeast (about 2¼ teaspoons)
2 tbsp. butter, softened
1 tbsp. granulated sugar
1 tbsp. garlic paste
2 tsp. dried dill
2 eggs, divided
6½ to 7 cups bread flour
1 tbsp. sea salt
½ cup grated Parmesan cheese

Preheat oven to 250°F. The stovetop will be a warm place to let the dough rise. Spray (2) 9x5-inch loaf pans with nonstick pan spray; set aside.

Place cauliflower, milk, yeast, butter, sugar, garlic, dill, 1 egg, 6½ cups flour and salt on top of flour in electric mixer bowl. Mix on low speed with paddle, adding more bread flour if dough sticks to sides of bowl. The dough should feel moist, but not stick to bowl. Continue to mix on low for 5 to 6 minutes or until dough looks smooth, but elastic. Divide dough in half and place dough in pans, pressing on dough to stretch and fill pan. Cover loosely with plastic wrap and place on top of warm oven; let dough rise 90 minutes or until dough reaches the top of the pan. Turn oven temperature to 375°F.

When oven is preheated, whisk the remaining egg with 1 tbsp. water in small bowl and brush top of dough with egg wash. Bake 30 to 34 minutes or until internal temperature is 190°F. Immediately remove breads from hot pan onto cooling rack. Let cool at least 1 hour before serving. Store bread in airtight bags.

Makes 2 loaves.

Creamy Mushroom Rye Bread

This recipe took multiple attempts to perfect. My friend and fellow pastry chef, Jeanne Kraus, suggested using cream of mushroom soup, since my first loaf reminded her of that flavor. I was not sure how the soup would affect texture, but it tastes great. And forget about multiple steps for shaping the bread. Simply place in the loaf pan, cover and let rise in a warm place for 90 minutes. The bread is great with hearty soups like French Onion or a beef stew, or makes a great Patty Melt sandwich!

2 tbsp. fat (bacon, olive oil or butter)
⅓ cup finely chopped yellow onion
2 cloves garlic, minced
1 pkg. (8 ounce) sliced baby Bella mushrooms, chopped
1 can (10.5 ounce) cream of mushroom condensed soup
1¼ cups warm milk

1 pkg. (¼ ounce) instant yeast (about 2¼ teaspoons)
2 tbsp. granulated sugar
2 tbsp. butter, softened
6½ to 7 cups bread flour
2 tbsp. sea salt, divided
2 tbsp. bread flour
1 egg

Preheat oven to 250°F. The stovetop will be a warm place to let the dough rise. Spray (2) 9x5-inch loaf pans with nonstick pan spray; set aside.

Heat desired fat in large sauté pan over medium heat until hot. Add onion and garlic; stir and cook for 30 seconds. Add mushrooms; stir and cook 4 to 5 minutes or until mushrooms are soft and browned. Remove from pan to cool; set aside.

Place mushroom soup, milk, yeast, sugar, butter, 6½ cups bread flour and 1 tbsp. salt (following this order, with salt last on top). Mix on low speed with paddle, adding more bread flour if dough sticks to sides of bowl. The dough should feel moist, but not stick to bowl. Continue to mix on low for 5 to 6 minutes or until dough looks smooth and elastic. Mix 2 tbsp. bread flour with mushroom/onion mixture to help absorb excess moisture. Add to mixer bowl and mix on low speed until mushrooms are blended well with dough. Divide dough in half and place dough in pans, pressing on dough to stretch and fill pan. Cover loosely with plastic wrap and place on top of warm oven; let dough rise 2 hours or until dough reaches the top of the pan. Turn oven temperature to 375°F.

When oven is preheated, whisk the egg with 1 tbsp. water in small bowl and brush top of dough with egg wash. Sprinkle bread with sea salt. Bake 30 to 34 minutes or until internal temperature is 190°F. Immediately remove breads from hot pans onto cooling rack. Let cool at least 1 hour before serving. Store bread in airtight bags.

Makes 2 loaves.

Pumpkin Cinnamon Pecan Ring

This beautiful, large bread ring is a showstopper! Make it the centerpiece for your next brunch.

Bread:
1 cup warm milk
1 cup pumpkin puree
1 pkg. (¼ ounce) instant yeast
   (about 2¼ teaspoons)
2 tbsp. granulated sugar
1 egg
4 tbsp. (½ stick) butter, softened
5 to 5½ cups bread flour
2 tsp. sea salt
Additional bread flour for dusting

Filling:
4 tbsp. (½ stick), butter, softened
½ cup granulated sugar
½ cup pumpkin puree
2 tbsp. ground cinnamon
Pinch salt
1 cup finely chopped pecans

Egg Wash:
1 egg
1 tbsp. water

Glaze:
1 pound confectioners' sugar (about 4 cups)
⅓ cup water

Preheat oven to 250°F; this creates a warm area on top of the stove for the dough to rise. Spray a 10-cup tube pan with nonstick spray; set aside.

Place milk, puree, yeast, sugar, egg and butter in electric mixer bowl and mix on low speed with paddle attachment until well-blended. Turn off mixer and add 5 cups flour and salt; mix on low speed until rough dough forms. If dough is soft and sticks to bowl, add more flour while mixing on low speed. The dough should feel moist, but not sticky. Continue mixing on low speed for 5 to 6 minutes until dough is smooth and elastic.

Spray a large bowl with nonstick spray and place dough in bowl; cover loosely with plastic wrap. Place on warm stovetop 45 to 50 minutes or until dough is doubled in size.

While dough is rising, prep the following:
Prepare the filling by combining butter, sugar, puree, cinnamon, and pecans in a small bowl.
Prepare the egg wash by whisking the egg and water in small cup. Set aside with a pastry brush.

Once dough has risen, turn off oven and place an empty large roasting pan in bottom of oven. Remove dough from bowl, place on lightly floured work surface and punch down dough to remove excess gas. Stretch and shape the dough into a large ball; cover with plastic wrap and let rest 10 to 15 minutes. This step will make the final shaping much easier.

Roll out dough to ¼-inch thick and into large rectangle. Brush edges with egg wash. Gently press filling across dough, leaving about 1-inch border on all sides of dough. Starting at one long side, roll up dough, jelly-roll style and press edges to seal; keep seam side down on surface. Using a metal bench scraper or sharp knife, cut dough lengthwise into (3) pieces, leaving one end (about 1-inch) uncut to keep pieces attached. Turn dough pieces filling side up and braid.

Transfer braided dough to prepared pan, wrapping around the tube and pinching together the end seams. Egg wash dough and place in warm oven. Fill roasting pan with hot water (adds humidity to oven). Let dough rise until almost doubled, about 30 minutes. Remove both tube pan and roasting pan from oven; preheat to 350°F. Leave tube pan on top of warm oven to keep dough rising. When oven is ready, gently egg wash dough again.

Bake 20 minutes, then cover pan with foil to keep top of dough from overbrowning. Bake another 20 minutes or internal temperature reaches 185°F. Immediately invert pan and turn out bread onto cooling rack. Prepare the glaze by whisking the confectioners' sugar and water in small bowl. Use the whisk to drizzle glaze over warm bread. Let bread cool completely before serving.

Makes 1 large loaf.

Roasted Garlic Bread

Roasting the garlic takes a little time, but it's well worth the effort! This flavorful bread makes the whole house smell wonderfully of garlic! It makes a great sandwich bread.

1 head garlic
Olive oil
¼ pound (1 stick) butter, softened
2½ cups warm milk
1 pkg. (¼ ounce) instant yeast (about 2¼ teaspoons)
1 tbsp. granulated sugar
5½ cups bread flour
2 tsp. sea salt
1 egg

Preheat oven to 350°F. Cut off top of garlic head to expose garlic cloves. Place in a large piece of aluminum foil and drizzle about 1 tsp. olive oil on top. Wrap garlic and bake for 45 to 55 minutes. Remove from oven and let garlic cool 5 to 10 minutes. Reduce oven to 250°F. Separate garlic cloves and squeeze out all softened garlic into a small bowl. Place butter and roasted garlic in food processor and pulse to break down garlic and blend well with butter; set aside.

Place milk, yeast, sugar and garlic butter into electric mixer bowl. Add 5 cups flour and salt. Mix on low speed with paddle attachment, adding more flour if dough sticks to sides of bowl. Continue to mix on low for 7 to 8 minutes or until dough looks smooth and feels soft. Spray a medium bowl with nonstick cooking spray and place dough in bowl. Cover loosely with plastic wrap and place on top of warm oven; let dough rise 45 to 55 minutes or until doubled in size. Turn off oven and place a deep roasting pan in bottom of oven.

Remove dough from bowl, place on lightly floured work surface and punch down dough to remove excess gas. Divide dough in half and stretch each into a ball; cover with plastic wrap and let sit for 10 to 15 minutes. Meanwhile, whisk the 1 egg with 1 tbsp. water in small bowl; set aside.

Spray (2) 9x5-inch loaf pans with nonstick cooking spray. On lightly floured surface, punch dough down into a rough rectangle. Bring up one long side to the middle and roll into a log. Place dough in prepared pan with seam side down. Repeat with second dough ball. Brush both loaves with egg wash. Place pans into warm, turned off oven (make sure oven is not hotter than 120°F or the yeast might become inactive). Fill the empty roasting pan with hot water (adds humidity to oven). Let dough rise 30 to 35 minutes. Remove from oven; remove pan with water from oven as well.

Preheat oven to 400°F. Brush top of each bread again with egg wash. Bake loaves 25 to 30 minutes or until internal temperature reaches 190°F. Immediately remove breads from hot pans onto cooling rack. Let cool at least 1 hour before cutting. Store bread in airtight bags.

Makes 2 loaves.

Spinach Potato Bread

This bread is great with any type of meal, but also makes a delicious sandwich.

1 pkg. (10 ounce) frozen, chopped spinach, thawed
⅔ cup roughly mashed, cooled, peeled baked potato
2 cups warm milk
1 pkg. (¼ ounce) instant yeast (about 2¼ teaspoons)
2 tbsp. olive oil
1 tbsp. honey
1 tbsp. garlic paste or finely chopped garlic
6½ to 7 cups bread flour
4 tsp. sea salt
1 egg

Preheat oven to 250°F. The stovetop will be a warm place to let the dough rise.

Place spinach in food processor (do not squeeze out water) and pulse to finely chop spinach. Add potato and pulse to combine well; set aside.

Place milk, yeast, oil, honey, garlic paste and spinach/potato, 6½ cups flour and place salt on top of flour. Mix on low speed with paddle, adding more flour if dough sticks to sides of bowl. Continue to mix on low for 5 to 6 minutes or until dough looks smooth and feels elastic. Spray a large bowl with nonstick cooking spray and place dough in bowl. Cover loosely with plastic wrap and place on top of warm oven 45 to 55 minutes or until dough is doubled in size. Turn off oven and place a deep roasting pan in bottom of oven.

Remove dough from bowl, place on lightly floured work surface and punch down dough to remove excess gas. Divide dough in half and stretch each into a ball; cover with plastic wrap and let sit for 10 to 15 minutes. Meanwhile, whisk the 1 egg with 1 tbsp. water in small bowl; set aside.

Spray (2) 9x5-inch loaf pans with nonstick cooking spray. On lightly floured surface, divide each dough ball into (3) smaller balls. Place the (3) balls of dough in prepared pan. Repeat with second dough ball. Brush both loaves with egg wash. Place pans into warm, turned off oven (make sure oven is not hotter than 120°F or the yeast might become inactive). Fill the empty roasting pan with hot water (to add humidity to oven). Let dough rise 30 to 35 minutes. Remove from oven; remove pan with water from oven as well. Keep loaf pans on top of oven to keep rising.

Preheat oven to 375°F. Brush top of each bread again with egg wash. Bake loaves 30 to 35 minutes or until internal temperature reaches 190°F. Immediately remove breads from hot pans onto cooling rack. Let cool at least 1 hour before serving. Store bread in airtight bags.

Makes 2 loaves.

Sweet Potato Cranberry Pecan Bread

1 cup warm milk
1 pkg. (¼ ounce) instant dry yeast (about 2¼ teaspoons)
½ cup granulated sugar
¼ pound (1 stick) butter, softened
2 eggs
⅓ cup sweet potato puree
3 to 3½ cups bread flour
2 cups whole wheat flour
2 tsp. salt
1 cup dried cranberries
1 cup chopped pecans
1 egg

Heat oven to 250°F. The stovetop will be a warm place to let the dough rise.

Place milk, yeast, sugar, butter, eggs, puree, 3 cups bread flour, wheat flour, and salt in electric mixer bowl. Using the paddle attachment, mix until well-combined and all the flour is absorbed. Continue mixing on low speed, adding a little bread flour if dough begins to stick to bowl. Mix 5 to 6 minutes, or until smooth and elastic. Add cranberries and pecans; beat to mix well into dough.

Spray a medium bowl with nonstick spray and place dough in bowl and cover loosely with plastic wrap. Place on warm stovetop 50 to 60 minutes or until dough is doubled in size. Turn off oven and place a deep roasting pan in bottom of oven.

Remove dough from bowl, place on lightly floured work surface and punch down to remove excess gas. Divide dough in half and stretch each into a ball; cover with plastic wrap and let sit for 10 to 15 minutes. Meanwhile, whisk the 1 egg with 1 tbsp. water in small bowl; set aside.

Line a large sheet pan with parchment paper. On the lightly floured surface, press dough down into a rough rectangle. Roll dough into a log. Place on sheet pan with seam side down. Repeat with second dough ball. Brush both loaves with egg wash. Place sheet pan into warm oven (make sure oven is not hotter than 120°F or the yeast might become inactive). Fill the empty roasting pan with hot water (adds humidity to oven). Close oven and let dough rise 30 to 35 minutes. Remove from oven; remove pan with water from oven as well.

Preheat oven to 375°F. Slash the top of each bread, using a sharp knife and gently brush on another egg wash. Bake loaves 40 to 45 minutes or until internal temperature reaches 185°F. Immediately remove breads from hot pan onto cooling rack. Let cool at least 1 hour before serving. Store bread in airtight bags.

Makes 2 loaves.

Tomato Herb Bread

Use tomato juice without additives for the best flavor.

1½ cups tomato juice, warmed to 115°F
1 pkg. (¼ ounce) instant yeast (about 2¼ teaspoons)
2 tbsp. granulated sugar
2 tbsp. olive oil
2 tbsp. Italian seasoning
1 egg yolk
3½ to 4 cups bread flour
1½ tsp. sea salt
1 egg

Preheat oven to 250°F; this is to create a warm area on top of the stove for the dough to rise.

Place juice, yeast, sugar, oil, seasoning, yolk, 3½ cups flour, and salt in an electric mixer bowl. Beat on low with paddle attachment, adding more flour if dough is soft and sticks to bowl. Continue beating on low about 5 to 6 minutes or until dough is smooth and elastic.

Spray a medium bowl with nonstick spray and place dough in bowl; cover loosely with plastic wrap. Place on warm stovetop about 45 to 50 minutes or until dough is doubled in size. Turn off oven and place a deep roasting pan in bottom of oven.

Remove dough from bowl, place on lightly floured work surface and punch down dough to remove excess gas. Stretch dough into a ball; cover with plastic wrap and let sit for 10 to 15 minutes. Meanwhile, whisk the 1 egg with 1 tbsp. water in small bowl; set aside.

Spray a 9x5-inch loaf pan with nonstick cooking spray. On lightly floured surface, punch dough down into a rough rectangle. Bring up one long side to the middle and roll into a log. Place in prepared pan with seam side down. Brush loaf with egg wash. Place pan into warm, turned off oven (make sure oven is not hotter than 120°F or the yeast might become inactive). Fill the empty roasting pan with hot water (to add humidity to oven). Let dough rise 30 to 35 minutes. Remove from oven; remove pan with water from oven as well.

Preheat oven to 375°F. Brush top of bread again with egg wash. Bake loaf 30 to 35 minutes or until internal temperature reaches 190°F. Immediately remove bread from hot pan onto cooking rack. Let cool at least 1 hour before serving. Store bread in airtight bag.

Makes 1 loaf.

Variation: Shape dough into two-ounce rolls and place on sheet pan. Egg wash and let rolls rise as noted above. Bake rolls for 12 to 15 minutes at 400°F.

Index

Page numbers in *Italics* followed by suffix "*p*" indicate photographs.

About the Author

Rose Deneen is a graduate of Le Cordon Bleu and has been a pastry chef for more than 20 years. Chef Rose Deneen has baked a variety of desserts at many restaurants and caterers in the Chicago area. She is an Assistant Professor at Moraine Valley Community College in Palos Hills, IL and teaches Baking/Pastry courses. This is her first cookbook.

Facebook: Chef Rose Deneen   Email: food-is-fun@sbcglobal.net

CPSIA information can be obtained
at www.ICGtesting.com
Printed in the USA
BVHW06s1406041018
529228BV00003B/3/P

9 781595 986702